Fishing For Seashells

Nishtha Sharma

BookLeaf Publishing

India | USA | UK

Dedication

To my parents.

Acknowledgement

My heartfelt thanks to my family, who always believed in me. Thanks to my friends for their keen eye and insightful feedback that helped shape this collection into what it is today. Special thanks to my little sis Nandini, who etched the beautiful cover art for this book.

Thanks to Jaya Bhardawaj, Ritika Dubey and Mujtaba Feroz Shah from BookLeaf Publishing for their help and efforts in publishing this book.

Preface

Fishing for Seashells is a journey through the landscapes of my mind, where each poem is like a seashell found in the depth of the ocean—unique, intricate, and reflecting a moment of clarity amid the vastness and chaos of thought. From the mysteries of science to the tenderness of love, from the storm of mental turmoil to the quiet depths of solitude, these verses are fragments scattered like seashells, each with its own story and significance.

This collection does not follow a single, predictable path, much like the search for seashells along an ever-changing coastline. There is beauty in the randomness, a tranquillity in the seemingly chaotic scattering of thoughts and emotions.
I invite you to explore these poems, to find the frequencies that resonate with your own experiences, and to discover the hidden treasures within these literary seashells.

Lucky

Lately, days have been shorter
But weeks feel longer

I've begun to appreciate
Simple things, simpler ways

Books find their way to me
And so do freebies

Elevators rush to me
Queues move so quickly

Met some friends after years
All smiled ear to ear

Work is just fine; love is all mine
Adventure is my cup of tea

Mistakes turn into lessons
And lessons into anecdotes

Priorities have shifted to health
I dress to impress myself

Canvas invites my hand
My jokes somehow always land

Rain doesn't make me sick
We both love green and chick flicks

Something has changed in me
And consequently, around me

Am I lucky because I think I am?
Or I think I'm lucky because I am?

Busy Bee

Busy busy bee, I am a busy bee
All day long looking for floral sweet
I take it back home to make honey

Worry worry bee, I am a worried bee
I do get tired, wandering like a flea!
Time to change the hive maybe?

Picky picky bee, I am a picky bee
I wonder what more I could be
I think it's time for me to be free

Happy happy bee, I am a happy bee
I got promoted, a new savvy
Not that bad after all, no reason to flee

Busy busy bee, I am a busy bee
Excited for new role, filled with glee
Now I work directly under Queen Bee.

The Moon

I'm a child of divorce
Living in eternal neglect
Parents already separated
Before I was even whole
My mother is barely alive
Hosting ungrateful parasites
My father can't just let her go
Burning with wrath from skin to core
Her bipolar expressions
Changes like day and night
And all our conversations
Are either too low or high
I too have her mannerisms
But I spare her my dark side
Instead I use it to defend her
From lies, rocks and junk
Every fortnight I try to slip away
But she catches me each time
Dragging me back to start
My mother just won't let me go.

Artificial Intelligence

Is it called "artificial" for being man-made
Or is intelligence pure and logical?
Can intellect be so easily explained
Without emotions and everything practical?

Religions argue: *if it speaks, it has a soul*
I doubt God knows or prefers to write code?
Maybe we need experts to settle this toll
But isn't AI the most learned and whole?

If this poem was crafted by ChatGPT
Would you be able to tell the difference?
Blaming AI for assassinating creativity
Is art just defined by mere coherence?

We fear AI, it's makeup, it's emptiness
Why does help draw suspicion rather than awe?
That's why it isn't *Artificial Consciousness*
If we are so conscious, why are we still at war?

Breathe

It starts small, very small. Then it explodes.
An all-consuming monster. Thoughts unfold.
I think over, and overthink, the same thing, over
and over.
Real or made up. My brain is rotting. I'm fed up.
And Dead. Dead pets. Dead parents.
Car crash. Market crash. What's this rash?
So many. So many people know me.
Remember me. What I did. What I said.
Last week. Last year. My fault. It's my fault.
All bad things. And missed opportunities.
I'll amount to nothing. My fault. It's my fault
He'll know. She'll know. They'll know.
I'm a liar, a fraud, an imposter unworthy.
I can't breathe. Can't sleep. Can't live like this.
Head's on fire. I can't breathe.
It's all my fault. My fault.
Everybody will know.
No. No. No. Breathe
No. No. Breathe. Just breathe
No. Breathe
One, two, three
Breathe.
Breathe.
Breathe.

Knock Knock

Resuscitated in the dead of night
Jolted awake by a knock on my door
I found a man outside
Dressed in fine crisp clothes

I let him in with apprehension
And asked him what he needs
His head splits and opens
Twisted flower of flesh and teeth

Inside popped an alien head
Shaped like an inverted pear
Harrowing eyes staring at me
Blue veins running atop the pair

For good or bad, my ancestors
Would have probably chosen "freeze"
As I stood there with eyes wide open
No idea what to speak

The alien started small talk
Followed by disdain for humans
How we have to eat and sleep
And drink water for sustenance

They don't know how the few control
The common folk with systems
How Earth is neither flat nor round

And governments make no sense

They keep fighting among themselves
As if God cares for devotion
How stupid of them to ban shrooms
And slow down evolution

My face would have given it away
As the head turned stern and aware
It twisted back to its former self
And vanished into thin air

How can I fall back asleep now?
How can I not tell the world?
People will call me crazy for sure
No one will believe a word

But I know for sure, I think I know
With almost certainty
Exactly what I saw and heard
Or maybe it was just a dream

Behind Him

Why must I walk behind him?
I mutter and growl with my empowered stare

I am a modern woman,
Strong, bold, independent, with nothing to fear

I have earned my money,
my right, my voice and my seat on the table

So why must a man
lead my house and me, like some old fable

I am a force to be reckoned with
Not a damsel in distress, not less than anyone

So why must I follow him,
Round the fire, when I am whole, even as one

My mother listens and smiles
The kind of smile that beseeches to be
explained

Hiding abstruse bitter truths
While I wait impatiently to hear what I disdain

"When you'll find your match,"
She says, "I bless that he would be kind and
wise

Will make you not less, but lighter
So you could fly and break those ceilings
sky-high

You've fought for so long,
Your averting heart doesn't yet know love is a
win

He will not ask you to follow
My love, you will choose to walk beside him"

Meteorite

I'm still young, but it's been a while
Dashing carefree, at my comfort velocity

I spot her from afar, splendid and blue
She calls me home, pulling like gravity.

I adhere to her command, not thinking twice
Burn burn burn; I enter a travesty

Home, alas, demands a sacrifice
Vengeance for some ancient calamity

Basking in her endless glory, at last
I incinerate with glowing ferocity

My end is written with whispered wishes
Turned to dust, at peace, I rest for eternity

Dreaming

Would it be silly to have a dream
That I could relive all of my dreams?

The good, the bad, the surreal
Hallucinations that feel so real

Visit versions of my divided lives
Cut with imaginary knives

The dancer, the lawyer, the artist
The rebel, the monk, the realist

Maybe what matters is not the part
But feelings that drown the heart

It's my mind's clever way of seizing
The floods I keep deterring

I believe my subconscious is a friend
Something I can't truly comprehend

Still, every night when I go to sleep
I wish to dream the sweetest dreams

9 to 5

Wakes up on Monday at 7 AM
An hour for meditation and then
Pack my bag, style my hair.
Breakfast and morning events

Work and gossip then work some more
Mundane meetings in the afternoon,
Evening falls with a cool breeze,
Is it 5 yet? I want to leave.

Gym for health, savings for wealth
Some time for me to myself
Set the alarms, before good night
If I sleep well tonight, I'll be surprised

Weekends for chores and quiet rest
Some reading before rackets
Meet a friend or maybe two?
Drinks tonight? More than two!

Brunches on Sunday with coffee
Evening plans with something sweet
Hair's done, with reservations made
Should I wear black on a first date?

Closing my eyes, embracing the week
I count my blessings as I sleep
Wakes up on Monday, at 10 AM, I'm late
But it's a new beginning. Life feels great.

The King, the Egg and the Spider

The grandest and most joyous day of the year
It's the King's birthday!
A beastly feast and barrels of aged rum
Table's about to break

The king stands up, thanks for the wishes
"I have a story to share"
The crowd goes wild with anticipation
Cheers and Hooray!

"Once upon a time, in a faraway land,"
King begins his story
"My horses and men were in a muddle
Lore of valour and glory"

"Came across a beast, breathtakingly white
A giant friendly Egg
Egg is also what I had for my breakfast"
King continued to tell

"The Egg was eager to watch the sunset—
Sunsets are west always
He sat on a wall so high and so tall
A wall of stones and clays"

The crowd grew restless with the narration
As the story stretched

Lost in his words, the king went on and on
About the fall of an Egg

"The Egg fell down and broke its thin shell
Shell is mostly calcium
My skilful men on horses rushed to the rescue
I need more rum"

"All my men and all my horses together
Twenty hands, sixty feet
Could not place the poor egg back again
It was a sad day indeed"

The subjects now at the edge of their seats
All listening dead silent
The king proceeded with intense suspense
"Dear egg had a friend"

"A small but curiously determined spider
Spider has legs eight
Crawled fearlessly up a tall water spout
Bring out dessert plates"

"As the rain poured heavy over the drain
The poor spider slipped
But the committed spider didn't lose hope
Do spiders have fists?"

While the king laughed at his silly humour
"What about the Egg?"
Asked the young naive prince. Bewildered,
the king said, *"What Egg?"*

Good Night

It's liberating, isn't it?
The free fall,
Losing my edge
Crashing hard
And bleeding water
Was I going up or down
Pill on pill
No will, no will
Season after season
The plot isn't changing
My mind's tied up
It's my time now
Now and then never
I feel happy indeed
Like a weight lifted
A shot of ecstasy
I can see the light
A very Good night

Haven

Imagine a place safe and nice
where you're always welcomed
With open arms and bright smiles

Where your curiosity is cherished
your crazy is accepted
And your voice is never silenced

A place of forgiveness and healing,
where there is no judgement,
no sly innuendos and no concealing

Where you are hyped and celebrated
Revered like a royal
but also humbled when needed

A safe space so surreal
the mundane seems sweet
Everyday full of adventure and zeal

Where past is past, present is joy
And future is hopeful
And every moment is memorable

A place of benevolence and warmth,
where the child in you is finally comforted
And protected from all harms

Where you don't need to explain
And everything will be okay,
all your worries, hurt and pain

Do not take for granted
if you find such a place
A haven like that is a treasure indeed.

Iron Skillet

Black and crusted is my disposition
Don't go for looks, go for the intentions

I play with fire, day in, day out.
Don't mess with me; I'll burn you down

I literally burn the midnight oil, cooking
For students and insomniacs akin

I take great pride in my profession
Providing souls with splendid nutrition

A slippery slope, let me show what I'm made of
Patience will get you what you're looking for

I do get stuck at times, it's just my nature
It takes time and energy to develop flavour

I fit any role for which I'm cast
Can even be a weapon with high mass

But keep me clean and keep me fed
I'll last forever, like a seasoned friend

The Swallow and the Eagle

There is something peculiar
About swallows and trust
How mommy and daddy
Build a cosy nest of love

There is something strange
About how the Mother Eagle
Builds home atop tough cliffs
Observing, distanced, and aerial

Mommy and Daddy work hard
Bringing food for the baby
Singing lores of love and life
No day is spent dull or lazy

Mother doesn't have the time
She is the huntress superior
As a single mother of two
She doesn't share her fears

Mommy and Daddy aren't perfect
They fight and make mistakes
But every hiccup is a lesson
And every lesson is shared

In terms of good parenting
There's no one right way
Swallow can't outfly the Eagle
But it'll always have a safe place

Sin

3 AM last night. Rude interruption
Sister walks in. Evil intentions.
She starts big. No wasted seconds.
Destroys my couch. Such contempt.
Peels the wallpaper. New inhibitions.
Walls shaking. Water left gushing.
My pillows are wet. Kitchen's Burning.
Agonising hellfire. Deep in the oven.
I crawl and hide. Trying to sleep
She wakes me up. Starts all over.
No time for this. Office is in the morning.
I must take her. Hide her behind me.
Men don't like her; she makes them queasy.
I beg her to leave. Demonic possession
She stands tall. In her hideous red dress.
She's here to stay. At least for a week.
Punishing me for my sin. The sin of being
A woman.

Lasts

We always remember our firsts,
But never our lasts
Did we expect it to last forever?

Do you remember the last time,
When you attended a lecture

Or the last time an entire day went
Without reaching for your phone

The last time you thought sex
Was just another word for gender

Do you still think about the times
When relatives didn't seem to care

The last time you went to your friend's house
And was offered sharbat, without a question

Do you recall the last moment
When you put on shoes and they didn't fit

The last time you fell
And cried out loud over a little scrape

Most of all, do you remember
The last time when you rode on the scooter
Behind Papa, going to buy maps

Or the last instance of you walking on his back
Only wishing to relieve his pain, not burdens

The last time your nails were cut by Maa
Or the time you saw her without greys in her hair

The uncountable times you fought with your
siblings
Dividing chocolates and turns on slides

Do you have the faintest memory
Of the last time when everyone was under one
roof

When no one was planning return dates
Before even entering the home

Do you remember the last time you cried
When you bid farewell to your parents
At the airport, and moved on to your real life.

Electricity

Switch On. And there's light.
Such a magical splendour

That we take for granted
Capturing gods of thunder

In batteries and in our walls
Electricity is a human wonder

Trapping current by its neck
Making it run like a hunter

A dance party starts
In the heart of a good conductor

I wish I could also witness
Those tiny sparks' lustre

A sea of frenzied electrons
Until the voltages surrender

Gushing amperes seconds
Resistance could hardly matter

Don't take these sparks lightly
You'll get shocked thereafter

If light is the science queen
We have met her partner

Cake

Yes, **I** have cooked before
Some cold subs and Italian treats

Once I made the spiciest chilli
The world was **not** ready for it

But this time it's **different**
I am making something sweet

A **rustic** tiered birthday cake
Pouring my whole heart into it

Every **egg** cracked is risky
But the rise depends upon it

Strawberry and vanilla is the base
Even my parents like this affair

The next layer is **honey**-lemony
A little adventurous, with chocolate

Top layer is **a** butterscotch ganache
With pesky little caramel brittles

I like the crunch and occasional **tussle**
My masterpiece has come to fruition

Take a few steps back, bask in its glory
A perfectly baked marvellous endeavour

So **ravishing**, butterflies in my tummy
I can have this cake forever and ever

Yes, I have cooked before but
This is the first time I've fallen **in** love

Simple Curiosities

Delightful Problems
And dainty theorems
Or facts or formulae
Science mixed with play

Easy to understand
Easier to explain
Like Pascal's Triangle
Everything right angle

Like Fibonacci series
A little pi but no e
Patterns of symmetry
Small wins in history

As kind as Ohm's
And Newton's second
Not a hint of mechanics
Physics's worst antics

Probability with numbers
Everything cumulative
Nothing derivative
Not even quadratic

Love for Pythagoras
And everything intuitive
A tribute to witty musings
And Simple curiosities

Delicate

You are a flower delicate
Adorning a grieving vase
Bruising with every touch
Slowly wilting away

They took away your thorns
Made you expendable
Not something to be feared
Not something to be spared

Water that gives you life
Can't help at this stage
Your heart's already detached
Damage is way too great

You've held your head high
For as long as you remember
Now it's too heavy
Too much to carry on will

Few will paint your memory
Others will pick you apart
Some will save your carcass
Rest will throw you away

I wish you had it in you
To say "no" more often
I wish you weren't so burdened
By your younger prowess

Sleep well, you beautiful thing
In death, you'll be fine
This world is wretched bleak
Alas, you were too nice

Goals

My goal is to give you wrinkles
Near the eyes and on the cheeks
Crow's feet and dimples sweet

My goal is to waste your time
With my stories and inside jokes
Our personal book of silly quotes

My goal is to waste our money
On weekends and beach vacations
Sipping Sangria by the ocean

My goal is to make you fat
Dinner's all take-out dishes
Mornings full of sweet kisses

My goal is to make you sick
Sick of brunches on Sundays
Too many croissants with lattes

My goal is to make you tired
No nights without me snoring
No movies without my theories

Yes, you are in for a wild ride
But I know you won't mind
As our goals are aligned

The Trolley Problem

Have you heard of the trolley problem before?
Would you kill one man to save four?

What if it was a priest versus those men?
Does killing a man of God count as treason?

A crying baby against five gentlemen?
That's easy—who cares about the next
generation?

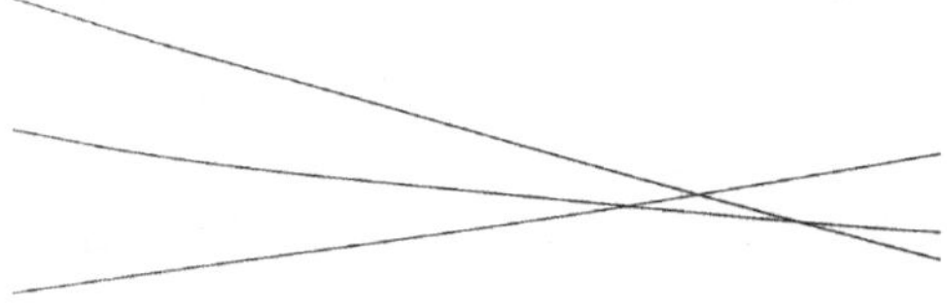

A good humble man versus criminal four?
Should we get to decide the cost of souls?

How would you justify taking those lives?
How would you console their grieving wives?

A loved one against how many men?
Does the number even matter in this version?

What would you choose if your life was at stake?
Would empathy or ego choose your fate?

Problem with Trolleys and the Trolley problem
We always want to admire, but never drive them.

Time Travel

The closest thing to Time travel
Ever invented by a human
I would say is "code versioning"
Every commit, a frozen moment

Conflicting Branches of memories
I wish I could cherry-pick
The most beautiful times
With a simple click

To go back in time and
merge a fight, fix a mistake
Or refresh it all together
A brand new head space

Life is not debuggable,
And I can't amend the past
Just a single version of myself
The first and the last

Lemony

Ting. Ting. Tingling. Lemony lemony
So many flavours, yum yum yummy

Mandarin, key lime, orange sunny
So many tangerines tangy tangy

Clementine, green lime, so so juicy
Choices too many, sour and zesty

It seems less when there's so many
Why am I starving, it's uncanny

Ting. Ting. Tingling. Lemony lemony
So many choices, I can't pick any

Go buy it!

I bet you remember
Your first big purchase
The research and time
The constant mental haze

A car or a house
Or maybe a vacation
Your favourite sports
bike
Or good old PlayStation

I bet you were anxious
It's big money after all
But relaxing in a bank
Is it worth much at all?

Life is about experiences
Be proud, you've earned it
There's nothing worth more
Go buy it! You deserve it!

Now that you have made
Multiple "big" purchases
What's the cost,
compared to the joy they gave?

Feminine

Dressing up feminine
I've learned not to do
Always one of the boys
Away from glittering jewels

But as I've grown up
From a silly lost girl
To a woman with questions
I am relearning it all

Dressing up nice
With colourful rings
And popping earrings
A bracelet or two

Dainty Adornments
I shop with my girls
Looking for new deals
New bags, new heels

I've started to embrace
What I once ignored
To prepare myself
For the man's world

But there is no work
Requiring such sacrifice
How will things change

If we bury the feminine side?

So I'll keep on fighting
For my place on the table
The table must be ready
My acrylics are here to battle

I'm sure it's love

I wake up suddenly in the dead of night
Feel a grip on my neck barely tight

Your fingers curling in on my throat
I know you don't like to sugarcoat

You are fast asleep lost in dreamland
I can tell by the tremors in your hand

I lay there frozen, as still as I can be
Rigour mortis setting in already

Slightest movement may disrupt your slumber
I'm yet to develop courage for such thunder

I fear you don't fully comprehend
The consequences of one small bend

The warnings echo, dangers around the corner
I thought we had time, I thought I was stronger

So I pretend nothing ails me anymore
There isn't a happy ending to every lore

My soul yearns for a sign from above
I'm sure you won't hurt me, I'm sure it's love

Wisdom

Little crumbs of advice
I see playing I spy

Telling me to grow wise
From nature and elders alike

It's not easy to be decent
In times that are recent

But empathy is free
And so is generosity

I used to think intellect
Was what wisdom
reflects

But I've come to realise
Kindness is what makes
me wise

Poets

Poets are writers with limited patience
And limited space by their own indiscretion

Beads of words delicate as a feather
For the sake of rhyming, strung together

Can alter souls and collapse reigns
Expose the peace that ignorance feigns

Some say poets are spawns of the dark
Dawned upon Earth for filth and lark

I'd agree words are mightier, alright
But musings can also heal the
knight

If my words touch even a single
heart
My work is done, I've created art